JOB HUNTING REVOLUTION

C.V BRANDING

Tolu Ogunyemi

TeamWork Print

This work is dedicated to all job seekers across the cities of Africa

CONTENTS

INTRODUCTION

Recruiters are faced with the task of reviewing hundreds of CVs.
From experience, when reviewing hundreds of CVs that look
basically the same, unconsciously, what you will start looking
out
for are the differences.

The moment you look similar to others, you lose to the
competition. Instead of looking the same as others candidates,
find a way to show to the recruiter that you are a superior candidate. My idea of a superior candidate is the one which has already
solved similar problems, the employer's current issues. By this,
the employer will rightly see you as the ideal candidate for the
job, you will stand head and shoulders above the other candidates.

The best and only way to achieve this is by showing to the recruiter your "wow factors". What I am asking you to do here is
to brand your CV more on your differentiation, rather than your
qualification. I mean you should not brand yourself as qualified.
Going by the competition in the employment market, employers
now have more qualified candidates than the vacancy slots. So
being qualified is no more enough to land you a job, most espe-
cially when you are above the age limit.

To achieve this, you must first find out the employer's priority issues and then use value statements to highlight how you have solved similar problems either for previous employers or in the cause of your life experience.

Your success as a job hunter depends largely on the quality of your CV. It determines the first impression an employer will have about you. So, it is very necessary you have an impressive CV. One key that I have observed lately that sells a CV to recruiters is Value Statement, but it appears that most, if not all, job hunters are ignorant of this key factor. I hardly see them implementing value statement in their CV.

What we have been taught is to state our career objectives and list our qualifications and skills. I am going to be talking here about what I call 'Value Statement' and how you can use it to brand your CV. What I am to reveal to you now is a new job-seeking skill not too known by most job hunters.

On average of ten per month, I do receive CV from job seekers, and going through all the CVs I have gotten over a year now, only one of them bears the touch of excellence that could easily attract the interest of a potential employer. What I see on almost all of them is a general career objective.

A career objective is an orientation to the prospective em- ployer as to what your expectation from his/her organization is, why he/she is receiving your CV. It is a feature every job applicants love to put on their CV. It is usually the first piece of information the employer sees on the CV, and draws the interviewer's atten- tion.

Career objective became a standard element of traditional CV when the demand for job candidates was more than the supply.

Then, it was possible for a job seeker to have multiple job offers. Because of this job surplus, employers devised career objective as a means of selling themselves as a best place for the prospect to work. Career objective allows the job seekers to pre-inform the employer what s/he expects from the organization.

But now, one thing has changed in the employment market, job shortage has replaced candidate shortage. The supply of candidates into the employment market is now far higher than the demand. Else, employers no longer care about what you want, instead, they now focus on what you can offer, the kind of value you can add to the organization.

When you start your CV with a career objective statement, employers see you as being interested in your own want, not the employer's needs. Because the market is highly competitive, because there are thousands of qualified candidates competing with you for the job, your interest does not really matter to the employer, until the hiring decision has been made and they are ready to make you an offer. What matters to them at the point of screening and interview is what you have to offer them, not what they have to offer you. So, you must learn to change your career objective statement to value statement.

Value statement helps you to clearly show to the employer the Return On Investment (ROI) your employment might possibly-give to the organization.

Do I need to say much about this career objective? No! I believe you all have a career objective written on your CV.

Employers these days are put off by career objectives. What I see people writing are boring, repetitive, lacking in originality, phony, irrelevant career objectives. The truth is most employers do not place any value or trust in Career objectives anymore, because they have read a similar objectives in a thousand other CVs. Check around, what you will see is a career objective copied from a common CV template, then it has become a general career objective that is too vague.

WHAT IS A VALUE STATEMENT?

In addition to your career objective, you should add at least one value statement to your CV that is if you must write a career objective. Else, you should totally replace your career objective with a value statement. A value statement informs the employer who you are, the kind of job you are looking for and it displays your personality and potential and puts flesh on your otherwise slim CV.

You can call it a Value Preposition **OR** USP (Unique Selling Point).

To have better undertaking of this idea I am putting to you, let us look at how Investopedia defines Value Statement;

"It is a business or marketing statement that summarizes why a consumer should buy a product or use a service. This statement should convince a potential consumer that one particular product or service will add more value or better solve a problem than other similar offering."

Now you have the idea of what I mean by value statement. A statement that proves to employer why you should be preferred to other candidates. If well-constructed, it appeals to the employer's strongest decision making drives.

CAREER OBJECTIVE VS VALUE STATEMENT

"To work in an organization that is target driven and goal oriented where innovations, creativity and excellence is their watchword."

"An experienced computer scientist with a successful track record of applying theory to provide practical solutions to organizational problems."

Please, tell me which of the two statements calls for your interest?

The first one is what we are used to, a career objective statement. It states what the candidate's expectation from employer is, it's more like telling the prospective employer - "see, this is what I am looking out for".

The second statement tells the employer whom you are and the value you are capable of adding to the organization. It is called a Value Statement.

Your CV should be targeted to the reader's needs instead of your own needs, your sales pitch, the first thing an employer should see on your cv aside your name should focus on how you can solve a problem for him/her. You will appear self-centered and selfish if all of your interest dwells on is what you want and does not consider the employer's needs.

As a serious job seeker, you should usually make sure that your CV is polished; with a simple and short introduction that can briefly inform the potential employers, what you do, your capacity plus the value you stand to add to his/her organization, going by your past accomplishments. You should ensure that the statement is relevant to the employer, closely related to the organization's activities, and attends to its needs.

It is often referred to as a "sales pitch" in the business world, otherwise known as your value proposition or a personal infomercial. It represents a quick synopsis of your background. It's a brief that explains who you are and what qualifications and skills you have.

I love putting it as a brief that shows what an employer stands to lose if the employment is not considered yours. How do you see that? Having employer to see what your worth is to his/her organization.

I bet you will become an hot cake in the employment market. This technique is commonly used in sales and marketing, and since your job hunting is all about marketing the brand called 'YOU', having a well written value statement is a good idea.

YOU AND YOUR CV

Now let's talk about you. - What is special about you?

As I said earlier, your CV should be targeted to the reader's needs instead of your own needs.

To do this, you need to know two things; what the employer wants and what you can offer. What skills and accomplishments set you apart from every other job seekers? You need to discover your hook. Once you know what you have to offer, it will be easy for you to tweak your value statement depending on the target and what their needs may be.

While you may need to look within for that value you can offer employer, you can only find out the employer's needs via research, informational interview and networking.

Take a lesson from the big brands ruling the market, like Coca-Cola, UBA, TFC, P&G, they found out what the market needs and decided what to offer before they created the products and approached the market.

If D-United didn't consider what to offer, they wouldn't be able to target the right market for indommie. This same approach goes to Job Hunting. You must decide what you have to offer before you hit the employment market.

What is the brand 'YOU' all about? What makes you special and unique? Think about what you can offer an employer. Consider your top five work and personal accomplishments. These are what I call values. Write them down and think them over. Think about what you want to achieve, your expectation from your employer that you call career objective. Then, tie your value statement with your career objective.

State the specific values about your skills and accomplishments that address the target organization's problems. Are they struggling with sales? Maybe you have a fantastic sales track record. Do they need new good accounting policy? Bring up your background and accomplishments in such profession. Brand yourself as the answer to their problem! Everybody wants to have someone who solves problems.

WHAT EMPLOYERS
MEAN BY EXPERIENCE

Most employ-
ers ask for experience but they are actually looking for values.
They list experience based criteria as a proxy for value, believ-
ing that by asking for experience, values will become apparent
in a few candidates, those are the candidates they refer to as
finalist - the shortlisted candidates. But job seekers do make mis-
take of over emphasizing experience over value.

By asking for your experience, what they are actually looking for are what you have accomplished and the impact those accomplishments had on your past employers. This can be tough for you to prove because you have been taught to list just your job responsibilities and skills.

WORKING EXPERIENCE - Experienced Vs Fresh Graduates

If you are job hunting with working experience, your value statement is best inputted in the working experience section of your CV. What is commonly written on this section of CV by most applicants is the name of the previous employer, period of employment, department and job descriptions.

All these only show you at your average, not at your best. Telling employers your daily activities does not make much meaning to the prospective employer like telling him/her how your skill better solved your previous employer's problem.

The hiring managers now seldom focusing on day to day activities or responsibilities, they instead look out for candidates who have already solved the organization priority's problems, who have created significant value for past employers.

WHAT MOST CANDIDATES WRITE BUT ARE NIT OF VALUE TO EMPLOYER:

This is what I see on most CVs.....

Company: XYZ Nig Limited
Period: June 1988 to May 1992
Position: Business and Financial Analysist Job
Description: Responsible for ....
If this is how it also appears on your CV, beautiful, you have succeeded only in advertising your former employer.
These are my observations:

Putting your experience in this format only paints you at your average not at your beat. Your CV is not a diary, it is a marketing tool, so it is expected to present you at your best.

What you did here is only showing your day to day activities. But employers seldom focus on day to day activities, or responsibilities. They are looking for problem solvers, outstanding candidate who have created significant values for past employers.

L-E-A-R-N

When you limit your experience to the description of your previous employer, department you worked with, and your business line, you are only describing your past employer, not whom you are. Recruiter can assume you are trying to use your CV to advertise your past employers. Your experience should be focused on you, on the values you added to your employers.

Compare this statement with the previous one;

Company: XYZ Nig Limited

Period: June 1988 to May 1992

Position: Business and Financial Analysist
Achievements:

> Acquired deep understanding of the Financial Analysis

wider role through work shadowing and training

➤   Increased the annual turnover of the organization by

17.5%

➤ Participated in several large projects leading to the improvement of business processes

➤   Brought about a dramatic reduction in XYZ average overhead expenses by 35%.

I want you to notice something in that value statement, did you see the 17.5% and the 35%?

This is the logic, monetize your achievement.

All employers have budgets to manage and financial goals to achieve. When you monetize your accomplishment by showing how much your input increased revenue, reduced costs, increased profits, you will appear superior to your prospective employer.

Money, financial gain is very important to all employers of labour. Such employer will see you as a good investment. I can assure you that every other protocols will be placed on hold for your sake. But in a situation where you are not comfortable or permitted to disclose the revenue or cost figures of your past employer, you can use percentage as in the case of the example given above, to demonstrate the value.

And if your value can not adequately be expressed by monetization, you can do that by showing your rate of performance improvement. Just ensure you find a way of using figures to express your value added.

For instance, a teacher can measure his/her effectiveness by his/her students' performance in exam with a variety of metrics to show the impact he/she had on the students.

HOW TO PRESENT YOUR EXPERIENCE AS A FRESH GRADUATE

What I recommend for you as a fresh graduate with no experience is what I call Competency CV. I always encourage applicants to apply for any desired job with or without experience.

Competency CV or better put, Skill Based CV is recommended when you have little or no relevant work experience. In place of your work experience, highlight your skill-based value statements. You can build your value statements around your value based activities in school, volunteer work, and club or association activities.

Check these out:

➢ Strong written skill as shown in my course work and project

➢ My ability to learn new skills quickly put me among the first set of students to work with the new database system in my degree course

➢ Highly analytical with strong attention to details achieving high grade in my Financial / Managerial Accounting

➢ Successfully carried out different roles with my team including those that required a practical task focused approach (certificate of excellence by club department if any)

➤ Worked with Rotaract Club Of OAU as project coordinator involved team training, budgeting and communication skills to coordinate students involvement and fundraising activities on campus. Raised N570,000 for our Help A Child Project.

GENERAL TIPS FOR EFFECTIVE VALUE STATEMENT

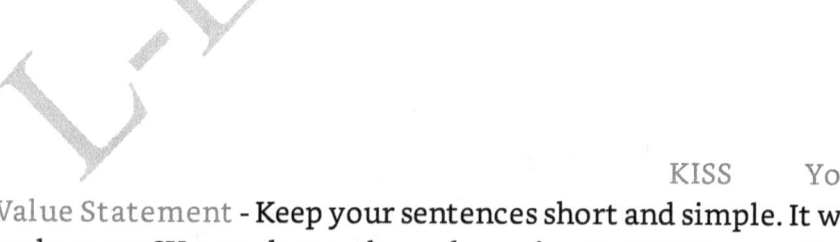

KISS Your Value Statement - Keep your sentences short and simple. It will make your CV sounds punchy and concise. By KISS I mean, Keep It Short and Simple.

Tailor it to what the employer wants - Let it show the evidence that you possess the required Skills. For instance, where good communication skill is required, you can say something like - "demonstrated good communication skills by the presentation I delivered at my school inter departmental debate".

Avoid introductory phrases like, 'part of my responsibilities ', 'I was nominated as '. Hit the nail on the head, go straight to the point. Put it like this.. 'Organized a symposium for my department with 650 participants in attendance'. They are interested in what you did, not what you were meant to do.

Use your professional master words when describing your experience and skills. It shows how professional are you with your job. There are a variety of ways you can describe yourself and your strengths. Try using the following:

'I am...'

Skilled at...	Excellent at...
A skilful...	Able to...

Competent in...   Very good at...
Extremely good at...   Talented
at... Familiar with...   Qualified
to...

Start each of your value statements with action words. This conveys your ability and power to achieve. Example of these words are; Produced, Initiated, Achieved, Analyzed, Created, Organized, Negotiated, Developed, etc.

Use the active voice, not passive voice. E.g increased revenue by 30%, not Revenue were increased by 30%.

Report the concluded events (like education, jobs) in the past simple, active voice. E.g: "Introduced a biometric system "
Use present perfect tense to emphasize your achievements. E.g, "this book has now been read by 100,000 students".

Use present continuous tense to report your ongoing study or activity. E,g, "I am carrying out research On ".

Do away with the personal Pronoun 'I'. Since your CV bears your name, the reader assumes you are the one talking, so there is no point saying 'I'. E.g., "I increased he revenue......" Better put, "Increased the revenue ".

Employers are looking for various qualities and characteristics in a potential employee. Use the following list of words to help you when describing yourself, whether in an application or at interview:

Able Accurate Adaptable Alert Ambitious Analytical Articulate Assertive Astute Bright Capable Calm Confident Committed Common sense Competent Computer

literate Consistent
Cooperative
Cope under pressure
Creative
Decisive
Dedicated
Dependable

Desire to succeed
Determined Diplo-
matic Diverse

Drive
Dynamic
Educated
Effective
Efficient
Energetic

Enjoy a challenge

Enthusiastic
Fast learner
Fast worker
Flexible
Focused
Friendly
Good communicator

Gifted
Hardworking
Helpful
Highly motiv-
ated Honest Im-
aginative Impres-
sive Insightful

Inter personal skills

Independent
Innovative

Initiative Intelligent Intuitive Keen

Knowledgeable

Leadership skills Loyal
Mature Methodical Objective Organized Patient Perceptive Persistent Polite Positive Practical Pro active Punctual Rational Reliable Resourceful Responsible Supportive Tactful Team player Tenacious Thorough Trustworthy

L-E-A-R-N

Versatile   Will-
ing

ABOUT THE AUTHOR

Tolu Ogunyemi

The man TOLU OGUNYEMI, a graduate of Banking and Finance, is a young visionary with great passion for training leaders and building entrepreneurs. He has taken his career in Intellectual Property Development (IPD).
Acknowledged as a foremost leader among his pears, he has played leadership roles in various capacities both while in school and thereafter. Over the years, he has been channelling his efforts towards producing vibrant, responsible generation of young people who are able to identify what they are cut out for. Tolu has featured as guest speaker at many trainings and workshops organised for students of several higher institutions, Youth Christian Associations, Corps Members of National Youths Service Corps (NYSC) and Business Leaders.

This and his exemplary leadership and inspirational roles have won him various awards in many Institutions of learning spreading across the country.

Tolu, who hails from Ekiti State, South West Nigeria, is the Chief Executive Officer of Mc. Kudos Enterprises, Promoter of Right Vision Multi-Concepts, and the convener of TeamWork Extra. Via these platforms, he has carved out his own niche in the industry as a Marketing Consultant, a Business/Inspirational Writer, a Public Speaker and an Inforpreneur.

Born on the 6th of May, asks Tolu what he likes doing most, he will tell you he likes listening to his conscience. Because of this one thing he enjoys doing most, he prefers reading and travelling, with his pen and jotter handy. Asked him why? He explained that reading and travelling gives him the inspiration to listen to his conscience and birth ideas that add value to mankind.

From this hubby of his, several books have emerged from his series of self meditations. Some of these books are; Gateway to Excellence (2007), Walking in Financial Freedom (2011), and this Spark of The Giants (2011), Fac.e-book Marketing (2011). In 2009, one of his books, "Gateway to Excellence" was approved by Ekiti State Government for the Senior Secondary Schools Students of the State Secondary Schools.

Job Hunting Revolution is recommended as a must read for every single individuals that aspires to be a Giant.